Aı

MW01290689

How to Master the Art of Analyzing and Influencing Anyone with Body Language, Covert NLP, Emotional Intelligence and Ethical Manipulation

JASON MILLER

Jason Miller

TABLE OF CONTENTS

Introduction 5

Chapter 1..15

What's the Problem? – How to Analyze People Instantly Using Proven and Successful Techniques 15

Chapter 2..26

How Many People Are Gifted with the Talent to Read People Instantly?...26

Chapter 3..40

Discuss the Different Types of People and How They Fit in the Social Circle. 40

Chapter 4..54

Basic but Proven Effective Techniques for Analyzing People 54

Chapter 5..78

Lies – Why They Affect the Way You Analyze People? 78

Chapter 6..94

Adverse Effects of Misreading People 94

Chapter 7..109

Analyzing Verbal Cues...109

Chapter 8: Looking into One's Own Self..........122

Conclusion...135

References 144

Introduction

I had grown up at a farm where my father used to have a herd of cows and buffaloes. We also had a garden of apples that we used to sell in the market to make our ends meet. Since childhood, I knew that I was a bit different because whenever I used to meet people, I immediately formed an assessment of them like what they are thinking and how they are going to talk to me.

One day I was walking down a lonely road along with my friend Jasmine. We had just returned after plucking apples from my garden. They were not for the market but to make pickles at home. Of course, they were not ripe. It was about the afternoon when we were passing across the graveyard. Not much of a haunted place like we see in the movies where the hero along with the heroine are caught by a witch, but enough isolated to send shivers down the spine of every sensible person. When we passed through this place while coming to the garden, the sun was shining bright with full energy, but now it was later afternoon. Also, the sun was nowhere to see as the clouds that seemed to be fragile at noon were slowly covering up the sky. Now they had turned into a thick blanket that wouldn't let a single ray from the sun touch the earth.

As we paced up, a dark and gloomy person appeared to be rising over the roof of a hut that was in the graveyard. I had a hunch that something was wrong. He had not seen us until now but could have if we didn't get off the track and hid behind the bushes. Jasmine wanted to stay until he disappears, but a powerful feeling had already gripped me that we must move on while staying along with the bushes. Of course, this made some noise and movement but I was ready to take the risk. We moved on and once we were past the graveyard, we ran on the way to our home.

When we reached home, we were perspiring and our heart was pounding in our chests. The feeling of how we got away and what would have happened if we stayed there or were seen by that person, would not let me sleep at night. That night it rained like madness. Even lightning struck some trees in the jungle and they were all roasted to the ground. I waited for the morning anxiously. At last, the sun had come out and we were ready to bask in its warmth in our yard. I had taken my breakfast and now I was getting ready to go out to school. It was then that I saw Uncle Tom running toward our house. He reached in a few seconds and broke the news that a lady was murdered in the graveyard by some unknown suspect. It all happened in the late afternoon.

The news crushed me and sent chills down my spine. The horror gripped me so hard that I was unable to speak for at least ten minutes after hearing that. I knew something was wrong with that person. He was giving off such a negative human vibe that I couldn't resist thinking that he was evil personified. Anyway, my hunch and careful reading had saved me. What if he saw us? What if he catches us? Could he have done anything to us to kill evidence for covering up his crime? Could anything have happened?

At that moment I didn't know what reading of people was. I just didn't know how we got away. But I researched the subject and brushed up my skills to be perfect in reading and to analyze people.

What This Book Has to Offer?

This book contains proven methods and techniques that can equip you with the skills to read people in an efficient manner. You can learn the skills and practice them to be an expert on how to judge people. When you have mastered this skill, you will be able to guide your behavior in accordance with how the other person is ready to perceive it. In addition, you will be able to eliminate any kind of misunderstanding that gets nurtured when you misread what other person means. Let's take a look at the chapters in this book.

- The first chapter will define what the problem is with reading people. You will be able to learn how to read people and how to react to them. You will learn the skill of analyzing the head movement and studying the feet movement. You will also get to know how you can avoid manipulation by detecting this kind of behavior earlier on in certain people.

- The second chapter will explain that people are god-gifted with the talent of reading people, but it also explains how you can learn the skill if you don't have it naturally wired in your brain. I have explained some tricks to integrate into your personality so that you can be able to kick off the learning process. Some of these tricks that you will find deeply explained are objectivity, ability to trust your gut and to find out how a person behaves naturally.

• The next chapter will explain in detail different types of people. The most prominent and discussed types include the joker, the loyal and the worker. In addition, I have explained different types of personalities like the observer, the idealist, the adventurer, and the performer. You will learn how a particular kind of person or personality behaves naturally.

- The fourth chapter hits the practical steps to reading people. You will learn how to read body language like the eyes, the hands, legs and arms. Then I will move on to the facial interpretation and analyze what facial expressions and micro-expressions to watch out for when you are reading people. You can take a notebook and write it down for reference when you are still in the learning period for reference. Then comes the turn of the inner instinct of humans and how it helps them walk safely on the road to success. The third section of the chapter will explain the importance of human vibes and how they affect our judgment of others. The human vibe can span around the eye projection, tone of our voice and the physical contact.

• The fifth chapter explains the types of liars and how you can efficiently deal with them. You will learn the techniques to protect yourself from their intentions and also help them mend their ways if possible.

• The next chapter sheds light on the adverse effects of misreading people. A flawed judgment can land our relationship in grave trouble. The chapter explains how we are prone to get confused by mixed signals and how they create misunderstandings. I have stated a number of examples about how a mixed signal can ruin our relationship. In addition, I have stated the signs to watch out for and how to react when you read a mixed signal. When you have read it, you will be better able to detect and analyze a mixed signal when you are confronted with one, and also act fast to end confusion.

- The second last chapter focuses on reading and analyzing verbal cues when you are talking to someone. It contains examples of verbal cues. Then it moves on from there to explain the difference between verbal and nonverbal cues. The chapter contains examples of a kid and a teacher and how they communicate through verbal and nonverbal signs. You can try it out on your own kids.

- The last chapter explains the importance of reading your own body language and looking into your own self. Unless you are clear about who you are and how you think, you cannot succeed in life. You will learn about the benefits of knowing yourself and concentrating on how your thinking flows. You will learn the importance of asking questions from yourself. You will learn how you can find what you like and what you dislike to make decisions faster. You will be able to know your own body's limits and how you are going to react to certain situations.

When you have read this book, you will feel yourself to be on top of every tricky situation. You will be able to judge people accurately and act accordingly. This book will equip you with proven techniques to analyze people and deal with them. This book is for businessmen, students, job-holders, spouses and almost all other categories of people. You don't need to have any special knowledge before reading this book. Anyone can buy and read this book and be a master of analyzing people.

Chapter 1

What's the Problem? – How to Analyze People Instantly Using Proven and Successful Techniques

By reading people, we don't mean that you have to read their minds like a psychic. Instead, you have to analyze their gestures and expressions to calculate what they actually mean. Reading people is about sensing their intentions like what is running in their heads through their behavior. If you gain this ability, you will be able to ameliorate your intimate and social life. When you have read and understood people, you can easily tailor your way of communication to suit their state of mind. This is how you can make an impact in a conversation.

Read People: Who They Really Are. How to Unmask Someone?

The best way to read people is not to let your emotions get over you. Forget about your past experiences. If you are trying to judge people by your past experiences, you will likely misread them. Pay detailed attention to their dressing. If they are wearing casual dresses like t-shirts and jeans, they like to be comfortable, so if they prefer comfort over hardness, they are unlikely to work hard and grow in a competitive environment. Also, see if they are wearing any pendants or stones. If they do, this indicates their spiritual inclination. This helps you judge in a better way.

Another important thing to take into consideration is a person's posture. A high head posture tells us that the person in question is highly confident. If he or she cowers, they suffer from low esteem.

In addition, the emotions that appear on a person's face tell a lot about it. Deep frown lines on a person's forehead suggest that the person is prone to overthinking. Similarly, if a person has pursed lips, he is most likely in anger and is harboring feelings of contempt. If he is grinding his teeth or has a clenched jaw, this means that he is tense.

Most people don't like to get involved in small talk. It is justified given the magnitude of our daily workload and the preoccupation associated with it. But if you ponder over it for a moment, you will realize that small talk, in fact, offers you a great opportunity to get familiarity with a stranger. You can read how he is going to behave in certain situations. That's how you are able to detect any abnormal behavior.

The Way You Treat or React to Other People Depends on the Way You Analyze Them

Once you have read people, it can greatly help you form your reaction to their questions or behavior. For example, if you have deduced that a person is highly confident and social, you will have to set your tone and posture to match his style. If he is confident but you are cowering, you two cannot have a healthy and productive conversation or collaboration.

Similarly, if a person has pursed lips, she is not in a position to listen to anything productive that you throw in her way because she is perturbed by something and will remain inattentive during a conversation. A person will only attentively listen to what you are saying if you are talking according to his or her mental state. If he is cowering and you are head high, he will feel intimidated by your posture and will not be able to open up his heart in front of you. The conversation is likely to end inconclusively or in a deadlock.

How Can You Be Accurate in Reading Someone Using Human Psychology, Body Language, and Personality Traits?

If you want to read people by means of their body language, you have to take a look at the cues that they share with each other with their gestures. Our face is one of the body parts that have considerable importance. Then comes body proxemics. This includes how your body tends to move in space. The third most important thing is body ornaments like your clothes and the jewelry you wear. Firstly, you need to decode a person's cues like interpreting the information that is hidden in their emotions and personality.

Look to Their Eyes

When it comes to reading other people's language, their eyes can be really helpful. You have to pay attention to their eye-contact and how they tend to look away while talking. If they exhibit the tendency to avoid direct eye contact, this indicates that they are not enjoying your small talk or serious discussion. In addition, this indicates disinterest and also deceit in some cases. You can also sense deceit if a person looks away or to the sides. If the person is looking down instead of looking straight, it means he is nervous. In some cases, it also shows submissiveness.

The blinking rate is also important when it comes to reading people's minds. Blinking rate increases when a person is stressed. When a person is touching his face during blinking, he might be lying to you. If the person is glancing at something, this suggests that he has a deep desire for that very thing. Similarly, glancing at a person suggests that the person desires to meet him or her or wants to talk to him or her. If he is glancing at the door, he desires to leave.

If a person, who you are talking to, is looking to the right and upwards, he might be lying to you. If he is looking to the left and upwards, he is speaking the truth. The reason is that it is natural for people to look to the left and upwards when they are using imagination. (Scott, n.d)

Study the Head Movement

The head movement of the person is also of great importance. If the other person is nodding his head when you are talking to him, it either means their patience or lack of patience. If the frequency of nodding is higher than usual, it is the indication that the person is fed up with listening to your talking and needs respite. If she is tilting her head to the sides, she is interested in your talking, but if the tilting is toward the backside, this indicates that the other person is suspicious or uncertain. (Scott, n.d)

Study the Feet

If a person is careful about his nonverbal signals, there is still one fragile point in which you can study to read what is running inside his brain. Why people miss out on controlling their feet is because they are too much focused on keeping in check their facial expressions and other verbal actions. Naturally, a person points his feet while standing or sitting toward the direction in which he wants to go. If he is pointing his feet toward you, he harbors a favorable opinion of you. If you are in a group discussion and a person whom you are talking to is pointing his feet toward some other person instead of you, this is a fair indication that he wants to talk to that person. One important thing is that feet movement and cues are meant to bypass other nonverbal cues. So, even if his facial expressions and eyes say otherwise, you have to follow the cues you pick by his feet.

How Can You Avoid Manipulation by Reading Someone's Mind?

Manipulators have one objective and that is to achieve their goals at any cost. So, their foremost weapon is using deceptive body language. There are some signs that people use when they are emotionally weak and are talking to stressors. But if this is not the case, they are very likely manipulating you by showing exactly the same signs. They will generally use these gestures to gain sympathy from you. Let's roll on to see what these gestures are and how can you avoid manipulation by reading them accurately.

They Will Rub Their Neck and Hands

When a person is manipulating you, he will rub his hands. This most likely indicates self-serving plotting. On the other hand, if he tends to rub his neck, this also signifies the same thing. The manipulator tries to gain your sympathy through this act.

They Will Stroke Their ARMS

When a person is rubbing or scratching his arms, he might have the full intention of manipulating you. This one is tricky because it is possible that the person has other reasons for scratching his arms such as hives. If scratching of arms comes in combination with neck rubbing, this may very likely be a sign of manipulation.

They Will Tap Their Feet

Manipulators tend to shift and tap their feet. This tapping and frequent shifting of feet indicate that they are impatient or even offended. Their impatience will compel you to make a decision in a rush that may most likely not be in your best interest. (English, 2019)

Chapter 2

How Many People Are Gifted with the Talent to Read People Instantly?

Reading people can be a god gifted ability and you can look for certain signs that show that you have that ability wired in your brain. Upon meeting a person for the first time, you usually have a powerful gut feeling which you just cannot explain in a rational way. You instantly form an opinion whether you like them or not. And, over time, when you get to know their real self, you realize that your gut feeling was right. People cannot always explain how they were able to judge others. It is something in their sub-conscious.

Another feeling that most people have but they cannot express is the power to know other people's thoughts. This also is a natural ability. More than once you might have noticed that you were able to tell what other people had on their minds. For example, you bring up a particular topic and leave your friend wondering because he was thinking about bringing up the same topic under discussion.

Sometimes you can accurately tell if your friend is upset. You don't have to communicate with them to know that. It is just his facial expressions that you have to study in order to reach a conclusion. If you are good at this, you have this talent as a god gift.

Some people really boast of their gut feelings. They are pretty sure of escaping dangerous situations just by following their gut feeling. You might have followed your gut and saved yourself from a dangerous situation. For example, your friends are planning a trip to a lake. You cancel the plan at the nick of the time and later find out that all your friends got injured in a road accident. Have you ever had that feeling?

Some people are naturally blessed with the power to detect if someone is lying to them or not. They can tell if someone is twisting the truth or is modifying it. Perhaps they fabricate a story for their personal gains at the cost of your benefit but they don't know that you are pretty good at finding out the loopholes in their stories. Their eyes, lips and hands tell you if they are telling the truth or not.

All the above incidents are pretty common to most of us. Everyone has a particular gift to use when he is caught in a difficult situation, but most people are unable to explain its words. It remains in their subconscious throughout their lives. If you are a Sherlock Holmes fan, you can understand exactly what I want to tell you. (How To Read People Like the FBI, 2018.)

Can Anyone Learn How to Analyze People?

The ability to read people is concerned with their gestures and other nonverbal signs coupled with their words. Well, it is a fact that you can have this ability in your genes, but this is something that can be easily learned. You have to memorize different signs to accurately judge what other people have on their minds. This includes studying, memorizing and then using a person's posture, gestures, voice tone, facial expressions and also the willingness for an eye-contact in the middle of conversations. There is no rule to read people because people are different. Some have mastered the art of becoming a conman while others appear to be wearing their hearts on their sleeves. You can easily tell what they are thinking and what will be their next step? (How To Read People Like the FBI, 2018.)

Some Tricks to Learn to Read People

It is impossible that you may understand the exact thoughts of a person, but it is always possible to read how they are acting. With the help of some psychology tricks, you will be able to learn how to read people.

Objectivity

The first lesson for a learner is to be objective. You must not let your emotions and biases cloud your judgment about a person. If you have already put that person in a kind of stereotype box, you are the least likely to be right about them. Think like a neutral person.

Try to Find out the Normal Behavior of That Person

When you are trying to judge a person, you should look out for his or her normal behavior. Sometimes you miss out on correctly judging a person just because the behavior he is exhibiting is his normal behavior. This can be scratching of arms, rubbing his hands or neck, tapping the feet and looking sideways. All these gestures, we have discussed earlier, pertains to some kind of nonverbal cues, but they can be a part of a person's normal behavior. That's why you need to set a baseline for that. Calculate what is normal and what is not. Biting nails can be common with a person and cannot always be a sign of lying. If you overanalyze, you can misread people and damage your relationship with that person. Scrape this gesture and look out for some other sign that crosses the baseline that you have set for that person's behavior. (How To Read People Like the FBI, 2018.)

Are you sensing any kind of inconsistency in that person's normal behavior and body language? If you are finding inconsistency in their behavior, phoneme can greatly help you reach the right conclusion. A phoneme is a basic unit of phonetics. If the person is lying to you or feeling nervous while talking to you, she will have an inconsistent voice tone. The pith in her voice will raise or lower down while she uses particular words. She can overemphasize some words to make you believe them. At this point, you are being manipulated.

You also need to understand the context behind the speech and gestures. For example, if a person is sitting with arms crossed, it can be a sign of unhappiness. But the person's choice of taking up this posture can be due to decreasing temperature in the room. Also, you should take into account the type of furniture the person is sitting on. If the chair has no arms, then the person will naturally cross his arms to rest them. When you are in the learning phase, you should broaden your field of focus. Focusing on just one body sign will land you in confusion, and you will misjudge the other person. (How To Read People Like the FBI, 2018.)

Trust Your Gut

Last but not least is that you need to trust your gut. Pay close heed to make sense of your emotions as well as feelings. You can tell that by studying how you feel when you meet them. (How To Read People Like the FBI, 2018.)

Is It Enough to Depend on Your Instincts When Analyzing People?

Whenever we are caught up in a difficult situation, we are repeatedly told and also we tell ourselves to trust the gut. This can be a bad situation or a bad person who we think is bent on doing harm to us. The gut factor jumps in to take its toll on our nerves. But for some people, gut feeling is so powerful that they think there is no need for reading people and analyzing body language. (Chu, 2017)

A single incident, a new employee, a new boss or a new job send the wheels spinning in our heads as we try to figure out how they will impact our lives. One reason behind this immense popularity of our gut feeling is that it is a simple answer to some complex questions that keep us awake at night. Answer to all questions is: "Trust your gut."

Let me explain and clear the confusion. Our instincts are not like a magic spell. We say a phrase and things start happening or an airy creature shows itself and fills us in about a particular incident or person. Instinctual feelings or intuition are linked to our past experiences and knowledge. The reason why people have different intuitional powers is that their experiences are different. The unconscious part of our brain starts working immediately after we encounter something new. It is like pattern matching. When we see a person smiling in front of us, our brain will match this sight with loads of data that is stored in our subconscious. Then it goes on to draw a conclusion. The process is so fast that the conscious side of the brain is totally unaware of this process. That's how we receive guidance in certain situations when we feel ourselves in danger. From this, we can deduce that if the experiences and knowledge are of greater size, our instincts work better. (Chu, 2017)

It is not enough to rely on your gut to reach a decision on whether the person is good or bad. What if you misjudge a person's intentions? When you realize his real nature, it will be too late. Take the example of a cop who, by nature of his duty, has to make fast decisions. He doesn't have enough time to scan through detailed information before he acts. So, one misjudgment can take the life of an innocent person. So, if we base our decisions only on our gut feeling, we are likely to end up making the wrong decision that could land us in trouble. The verdict is that you have to pair up gut feeling with the knowledge that you have about reading their gestures.

It is not always a good idea to follow your gut. Sometimes it is better to just eliminate the need for your gut feeling. You can do this by befriending someone and talking to them without heeding to your gut feeling. Your judgment ought to be calculated and well measured, and should be free of certain prejudices. Otherwise, you are highly likely to make a mistake and lose a friend. (Chu, 2017)

What Can You Do to Improve That Skill?

You can predict what others are thinking. You can read their minds, theorize what they are thinking and also understand their gestures. From all the data, you can know their intentions and analyze their emotions. On the basis of this knowledge, you can predict what their beliefs are and what is inside their hearts. All this makes your conversation with that person fun and productive. To achieve this feat, you should focus on brushing up your skills of reading people. Let's see how to do that.

- You need to stay focused and also be present in the current moment. Never think about yourself amid the process.

- You must be all ears to others. Listen to them attentively. Read between the lines, try to understand the context of their speech. Also, try to understand what they are not saying and keeping back. First, process their words in your brain and try to deduce their meaning. After that, you can respond.

- While you are communicating, you ought to study his facial features, his dressing, the jewelry and makeup in case of a female. Don't forget to take a look at his or her hair cut. In addition, you should take into consideration the surroundings where you are communicating with that person. To improve your reading skills you have to be efficient when it comes to studying that person's facial features and dressing. You have to invigorate your observation skills. You should not miss out on anything minute to large. Even a slight aberration in the person's hairstyle should click your brain.

- You should not lose focus due to some intrusive thoughts. Keep it on the person in front of you. Detect any nuance in their behavior and follow how it develops.

• To improve the skill of reading people, you need to stay calm. If something is perturbing you and you are not at peace with yourself, you will not be able to read the person in front of you accurately. Inner calm is directly proportional to focus. The higher the level of your inner calm, the greater your focus will be.

• If you are the kind of person who loses patience too soon, you are least likely to read and analyze other people effectively. Sometimes you have to listen to another person's blabber on end in order to get to know them better. Practice it if you lack this ability.

Chapter 3

Discuss the Different Types of People and How They Fit in the Social Circle.

All of us are full of different flaws that make us feel ashamed. We do have strengths that we want to brag about in front of everyone. Some of us prefer to stay natural in their everyday life while others love to take up their favorite persona to get through different hurdles in their lives. Some people like to make their way by deception, lies and manipulation while others prefer to face stumbling blocks but refuse to deviate from the right path. Whatever our choice of being a person in our lives is, the goal mustn't be of hiding our weaknesses as well as dark spots if we have any. We must allow our flaws to be a part of our personality. We should celebrate our flaws. This is what being human is about. When a person takes up a fake persona, he forgets that the people, who are loving him, are actually loving that persona that he has taken up and not that person who is in hiding under the fake personality. The real success is that people start loving us because of what we are and not because of what we are trying to become.

The Joker

The first category is a joker. The foremost feeling on hearing the word joker is of a person who is cracking jokes and laughing his heart out even during sober conversations. Jokers love jokes, costumes and makeup. Each makeover gives them a new look and personality. They love to hide their real looks and nature to others. Generally, jokers are considered harmless but if we bring to mind batman's joker, things get totally different. A scary and nutty person comes to mind who is evil personified. That joker is always bent on inflicting the greatest pain on the people surrounding him. Can you think of a person who fulfills the above personality traits? Do you know anyone who laughs too much, always cracks jokes or tries to tease others while laughing it out? Beware! Jokers are masters of disguise.

The Smart One

Smart people have the ability to mold themselves according to the situation. They learn or are naturally gifted to adapt to changing circumstances. Smart people always remember to read other people's styles to gain more knowledge about them. They tend to see through the motives behind their acts and also their hidden desires to work with them and gain benefits. Smart people are good at conveying their messages through in an effective manner and without making the slightest buzz. They know how to express their feelings in a clear way, which is the most important thing when it comes to building and strengthening a relationship.

Similarly, smart people are very successful in their businesses or jobs. They work hard to learn how to read people and the rest gets automatically easy for you. You can tell if a person is smart by looking at how they behave with you and other people around him. One important point to note is that smart people are very good at taking care of their personal interests, even at the cost of others.

The Worker

Workers are the people who belong to a specific social class that is known for doing jobs for low pay only to live hand to mouth in their lives. The jobs they do low demand skills and labor and also have low literacy requirements. This category of people also lives off on social welfare programs. Working-class people mostly remain preoccupied with their day-to-day expenditures. They don't have time to take up different personas and disguises. Also, they are not smart enough to get a job done in the easiest way possible. Their brains are generally wired to do it the hard way. These people generally wear their hearts on their sleeves. They are easy to predict and are simple to understand.

The Loyal

These people are hard to find but exist. They are reliable as well as truthful. If a person is loyal to you, he shares affection with you and will not leave you when life gets hard for you. Loyal people think from their hearts and always work for the benefit of the people who are close to them. Just like the working class, loyal people are easily predictable and trustworthy.

The Strong

Physically strong people generally have happy temperament. A strong person has higher levels of physical and mental strength. They don't have self-pity; that's why they are confident and good at judging people and dealing with them. Before they judge other people, they try to judge themselves. In addition, they have higher levels of self-restraint. Their nerves are powerful that's why they are patient. They also are good listeners and observers. Their physical and mental strengths make them very good at reading other people and reaching an educated judgment. They don't hesitate to ask for help when they are in need, and also, they are open to helping others.

Different Types of Personalities

People are driven by their nature when they do this or that and leave you wondering why they did something that looked unwanted to you. It is perfectly normal if you think you need to want to understand someone a bit more than you already do. This someone can be a loved one or a person at our workplace. We have to accept the reality that people are not perfect. We are different and it is this difference and diversity that makes this world a colorful and interesting place to live in. When people stay true to their role, they tend to contribute their bit to this diverse world. Just imagine if we were all created in the same way, how the world look would like then. It would be boring.

Take an example of diversity. When a car hits a motorbike in a road accident, a huge number of people gather at the site. Most of them are on-lookers who are just investigating what happened. Some mourn the wounds of the injured while some call the ambulance. Only a handful of them step up and actually help the injured recover their senses. They try to administer to the first aid and take care of them until the ambulance arrives at the site. It is not that those people leap into a house on fire without thinking about their lives. We react differently to different situations. These reactions are triggered by our fears and desires. Sometimes they motivate us while at other times, they just demotivate us.

In analyzing people, you should know the people around you. What they do and how they react to different situations. By knowing their personality types and the fears that guide their behavior, you can improve how you interact with different people. It helps you read people in a more efficient way so that your interaction with them becomes smooth and your analysis of people broadens and deepens. In addition, you can track down your own personality traits as well as faults. Let's roll on and take a look at different types of people in the world.

The Reformer / Idealist

The Reformer is a perfectionist. They have principles and are conscientious. These kinds of people have certain ideals to follow and they come down hard on themselves as well as on other people. They just love to keep them at pretty high standards. They are dedicated and responsible besides having perfect self-discipline.

They are usually successful in life because they tend to get lots of things to happen in a short span of time, and that too in the right way. They are always looking forward to setting themselves on the right path by eliminating their weaknesses. (9 Personality Types – Enneagram Numbers, n.d)

The Performer

As the title suggests, these kinds of people will always be setting goals for themselves. They are highly target-oriented individuals and they believe in doing rather than sitting on the couch and thinking day and night. They are always striving for success. This drive makes them pretty excellent at doing things right. You can find them in a big company, a shop or on the street selling vegetables or fruit. Wherever they are, their eyes are always on the horizon. They have dreams of success and they are in the world to make them happen. These kinds of people are considered as role-models by many other people.

They have their fears that drive them toward the top. What makes them perfect is their urge to become somebody. The fear of dying as nobody makes them state-conscious. Instead of discouraging others, they respect the opinion of other people. (9

Personality Types – Enneagram Numbers, n.d)

The Observer

This kind of people spend time on thinking and are of an introvert type. Their focus always is on gaining knowledge. They also prefer reading their own personality instead of reading others. They remain absorbed in themselves and love to play with different types of concepts. They usually abhor worldly attractions like big mansions, cars and social status. They are always busy in searching for themselves. They prefer to observe what is happening in their brains. You can see that these people will lock themselves in their rooms for hours as they love to understand how things go on. This exclusive behavior allows them to concentrate on what they do, that's why they are usually considered as experts on what they do. As they don't have the social skills that are needed to keep relationships healthy, they get overlooked most of the time.

The Adventurer

These kinds of people are fun-loving people. You will see them engaged in enjoyable pursuits and also, they are often in an upbeat mood. They thrive on pleasure and adventures, which makes them a really positive person. They tend to avoid negativity at all costs, which helps them fight off pessimism and stress really well. They are also very optimistic and don't let tough challenges mar their optimism. They are the ones who always find that silver lining in dark clouds. They stick to that silver lining and turn negative situations really fast and really well. (9 Personality Types – Enneagram Numbers, n.d)

Also, they are highly inconsistent. As they are fun-oriented, they remain in a certain work until the fun factor is alive but shoot out of it once they are bored no matter if the work is complete or not. Completion of projects poses a big challenge to them; that's why they struggle to be successful in the practical world.

The Warrior

As the name suggests, these kinds of people love to throw and take the gauntlet. They are strong and have dominating personalities. You can say they are born leaders and are really confident. They are real alphas. They hate to depend on other people and also don't like to reveal their weaknesses. Instead, they use their strengths to give a cover to those people who are around them as their family and friends. They are always ready to take charge of any situation no matter how thundering and dreadful it is. They love to be the masters of their own fate and they also prefer to take control of people as well as circumstances.

Their inner strength also makes them rigid, straight forward and sometimes haughty and harsh. They cannot tolerate signs of weakness in other people. They are ready to confront others on petty issues. They are always ready to express their anger and frustration on things they don't meet up with their expectations. These are the ones that are quite difficult to understand. Their nature is too intense and volatile to let others read them. (9 Personality Types – Enneagram Numbers, n.d)

Chapter 4

Basic but Proven Effective Techniques for Analyzing People

This chapter will walk you through some basic techniques for analyzing people. You will learn what body signs you have to read in order to understand what is running in the other person's mind. In addition, I will explain in detail the importance of gut feeling and the role it plays when you are trying to read other people. The chapter will also walk you through the importance of emotional energy in reading people.

I have touched upon the topic of studying body signs in the first chapter. This chapter will help you learn in detail what each body sign tells about a person.

Posture

How we carry our bodies speak volumes about our personality and mindset. The posture that we keep our bodies in tells a lot. I have earlier on explained what a straight posture indicates. I am going to add on to the previous information. When observing a person's posture, you should observe whether a person has an open posture or a closed one.

An open posture is when a person keeps the trunk of her body exposed. If you observe it in a person, she is likely to be friendly, willing and open to you. On the other hand, a closed posture is the one in which a person hides the trunk of her body. For example, she will hunch forward or keep her arms crossed. This is the opposite of openness, and the person in question will exhibit hostility and anxiety.

Body Language

Body language is the nonverbal signals that we send through our gestures. In simple words, it is about communication through our bodies. It includes our hand movements and facial expressions to as little things as our pupils. If we observe closely, we will see that people tend to give away a great volume of information through nonverbal signals. As I have already suggested, the key to reading nonverbal signs accurately is to take these signals and study them as a group.

The Eyes

Our eyes are considered as windows to our souls. They are the easiest to learn and most people can do that even without prior training. They tend to reveal a great amount of information about what is running inside our hearts. What we feel or think comes into our eyes. Even a naïve person can take the hint in the eyes of the speaker. But it is not just the eyes that should be studied. Pupils are also very important to know other person's minds. Look out for dilated pupils as they indicate increased cognitive struggle.

Pupils tend to dilate if they are looking at something they appreciate. This is not an easy job to do. If you keep observing different people, you will finally learn how to observe and detect any change in the pupils. If pupils are highly dilated than normal, it means that a person is attracted to someone and is aroused.

Hands, Legs and Arms

Gestures by hands, legs and arms are very important. I'll add on to the previously stated details. Gestures, like our eyes, carry plenty of information about our personalities. Our waving, tapping and pointing have hidden meanings that ought to be understood if you want to master the art of analyzing people. Well, it is important to sort out these gestures as some are cultural traditions like a raised straight palm. In some Asian countries, this suggests hello and in the United States, a thumbs up suggest that everything is fine. You have to keep in view these signs so that they are not mixed up with nonverbal cues.

Coming back to nonverbal cues. If a person has a clenched fist, this indicates anger but in some cases, this also indicates solidarity especially when shown by a politician or a public figure. For a clear analysis, you should study this gesture combining it with facial expressions and speech. Similarly, in some countries, people use the okay gesture that is formed by touching the index finger with the thumb. In some countries, this suggests that everything is going on fine while in parts of Europe, this means that you are nothing. In some Asian and South American countries, this gesture is considered vulgar.

Arms and legs are also quite useful in nonverbal communication. If a person tends to open his arms and keep it that way, he is an attention seeker and full of life. We have learned earlier on that crossed arms suggest closeness and defensiveness. A common gesture that you might have come across is the one in which a person stands with his or her hands on the hips. This is an indication that the person is fully in charge of circumstances and is ready to face anything. In rare cases, it may suggest aggression.

If a person clasps his hands behind the back, he is bored and anxious about something. We have learned earlier on what tapping our feet means. Besides, tapping your fingers also means a lot. It can be a sign of boredom or frustration. When a person crosses his legs, he is closing off on society and wants some personal space. He will prefer privacy than socialization.

Personal Space

More often, we are in need of personal space. Sometimes we want to mix up with people and party but sometimes we need personal space to breathe in. This happens to everyone. You might have been through the phase when you start feeling uncomfortable because of the presence of a particular person. In technical terms, this is known as proxemics. Anthropologist Edward T. Hall explains four levels of proximity between two people. Let's discuss them one by one. (Cherry, 2019)

Intimate distance: Ranging between 6 and 18 inches, this indicates that two people are enjoying a closer relationship. They are comfortable with each other. Two people come at this distance while they are hugging or touching each other.

Personal distance: Ranging between 1.5 to 4 feet, this distance suggests that two people are family members or close friends. If two people keep this distance but are comfortable in their interactions, this suggests how intimate they are in their lives.

Social distance: Ranging between 4 and 12 feet, this physical distance exists between people who have acquaintance with each other. With a coworker, the distance will shorten while with a person whom you don't know well such as a plumber, you will keep it at 10 to 12 feet.

Pubic distance: Ranging between 12 to 25 feet, this physical distance is used in public areas when you are addressing a gathering or a class or giving a presentation to your staff. (Cherry, 2019)

Apart from that, if a person comes closer to you, this suggests that he is looking for a favor from you. On the contrary, if the other person moves away, this means there is a lack of mutual connection between you two.

The above-mentioned distance is not something carved in stone. It differs in different cultures.

Mannerism

Winking is a normal act between friends and intimate people, but when a stranger wink at you, it appears invasive and offensive. Wink is generally a break in eye contact which suggests that the person is trying to disrupt the flow of conversation. On a lighter note, while cracking a joke, winking is absolutely fine. Winking without reason, tends to confuse the other person. So, steady eye contact is always the way to go.

If a person has placed his arms in an unnatural position, he is not sure of himself. He is not relaxed and is suffering from a lack of confidence. The conversation with an uncomfortable person tends to be unproductive and inconclusive.

Facial Interpretation

Reading one's facial expressions is an integral part of understanding his nonverbal behavior. We have already discussed some visible expressions like winking, blinking and many other expressions. In this section, I'll briefly discuss micro-expressions. They are brief and involuntary expressions that appear on a person's face. They have great importance because it is pretty hard to fake them. Let's discuss them one by one.

A person's eyebrows will appear to be raised with a slight curve. Their skin just below the brow will appear to be stretched. His forehead will have winkles and his eyelids will remain open for a while. His jaw will appear to be dropping and teeth will be slightly parted. Their mouth will remain normal with no signs of tension.

Pay close heed to a person's lips to detect the element of disgust in their disposition.

Look out for if their upper lip appears to be raised or upper teeth appear to be exposed. Also, see if his nose has wrinkles and cheeks, raised. Any such sign shows that the person is feeling disgusted.

You can detect anger from micro facial expressions. She has slightly lowered her eyebrows or drawn them together. Other signs of anger are tension in the lower lid or bulging eyes. In addition to this, if their nostrils are dilated or their lower jaw seems to be jutting out, this also shows that they are in anger.

You also can detect happiness in other people by observing their faces. She is happy if her lips appear to be drawn back. Similarly, if her mouth is parted and teeth are exposed, this is an indication of happiness. Happy people have their cheeks raised eyelids lowered with wrinkles evident underneath. Another common sign is the appearance of crow's feet on the outside of the eyes. An important thing to note is that if she is not engaging her side-eye muscles to show her happiness, her happiness is fake.

Inner Instinct

Inner instinct or gut instinct guides the physical reactions that we give to the world around us. It is the feeling that we sense when our bodies are responding to the processing of information that is stored in our subconscious, as I have briefly explained earlier on. The main purpose of our gut instinct is to give us protection in the wake of unusual circumstances. Sometimes people cannot define it but they are relying on it to deal with worldly matters. Their gut instinct guides them through thick and thin. Its power and influence vary in different people depending on their experiences and spiritual state.

Some people call it a hunch while others label it as an inkling, but in general, it is dubbed as gut instinct or instant instinct. This is different from intuition as it is our primal wisdom, while intuition is our spiritual wisdom. Both humans and animals have gut instincts. In some cases, in animals, this feeling is more powerful than humans.

Take the example of a herd of zebras. Even when they cannot see the lions that are lurking behind the bushes, they somehow sense their presence. When one of them whinnies, the rest of the herd starts racing away for cover. If you are fond of Animal Kingdom documentaries, you might have seen such scenes. Similarly, big animals like elephants rely on their gut feeling to find food and water resources.

If you are a cat lover, you can see that your cat will change its mind once or twice before it jumps over from the second story to the first story. Have you ever heard any story of hikers who got lost in the mountain trails? They had to navigate through the mountains without any compass or anything else to take help from. One of them had a hunch to go to the east and the rest of them followed him. In the end, they had successfully reached the camp. Just imagine what would have happened, had that hiker ignored his hunch.

Sometimes you have a strong feeling that something has happened to your son who is at home. You ditch the office and drive back home to find him unconscious on the floor. If you take a closer look at the world around you and also at your own life, you will find that similar incidents have been happening to you.

Signs of Gut Feeling

There are certain signs to watch out for if you want to follow your gut. The top indication is a sudden feeling of fear, especially if it is uncalled for or totally out of context. The second is a powerful urge to accomplish something just like an inner pull. You might also suffer from chills and shivers in your body. Goosebumps on your arms and body in combination with tingles up your spine also indicate that there is something wrong.

One important thing to consider is that signs of gut feeling differ for different persons. For example, some people may not experience any of the above. Instead, they get nauseous or have physical uneasiness. A few people tend to get alarmed at times while only a handful of people hear instructions or warnings in a clear voice. You might have one sign or all of them.

Discuss Intuitive Cues

Intuition means "to look within." Some scientists term it as sophisticated intelligence. People are viewing it as something that helps us make decisions rather than being a magical thing that cannot be learned. Still, the fact remains that ancient and advanced civilizations like Buddhism, Hinduism and Islam have connected intuition to the human soul. You can see if your intuition is at work by following some simple signs. You will start feeling light and clear in your mind. No emotions will affect your judgment and you will be absolutely calm and relaxed, and even inspired. If you are observing similar signs in your body and brain, your intuition is most likely at work.

Aha Moment

Things come to a standstill at times. A person who is running a clothing factory complains that despite producing the best garments in the market, customers are drying up day by day. He had run a marathon marketing plan to boost up sales but to no avail. Is more marketing the only solution? Shifting the production model can be a viable solution to the problem. Brainstorming new ideas and selling techniques is what we usually do to solve this kind of situation. But what if ideas just stop coming to us? What if nothing seems to be working? Maybe he should freeze for a moment and do nothing. Yes, this works sometimes. He should just stop pursuing a solution to the problem. Instead, he should take a shower, start playing golf or maybe watch a movie. People hit upon amazing solutions to overdue problems when they detach them from the current scenario for a while.

The key to reach the aha moment is creating an environment that is full of silence as well as solitude. These conditions are essential for your brain to nurture these moments. Ultra-quiet places are always the best for making better decisions. Once you have found a quiet place for yourself, you have to start looking inward. Focus on the live stream of thoughts. You have to detach yourself from the outer world like your cell phone and any other thing around you. When the external information ceases to reach your brain, you will slowly start noticing the aha moment. Gradually, you will achieve the "idle" mode of your brain. It is important to know that you don't have to stress out your schedule to get the aha moment. Instead, find a few quiet moments on a daily basis to do this exercise. Also, try to turn off all the electronic gadgets at least for a few hours in a day so that you can leave your brain to wonder for a while.

Human Vibe

The vibe we give off is equally important for reading people as reading their body language. This is closely linked to intuition. We run away from some people and try to be close to some of them. More often, we hear people say that they feel good or bad vibe by being around some people. Some people really elevate our mood when we are around them, while others drain us out of our positive energy.

The impact of the human vibe can be felt when we are just inches or feet away from a person. Some cultures like the Chinese dub this invisible energy as life force, named as chi. Let's take a look at a few examples.

Sometimes, your spouse says sorry to you but you feel that he is not really sorry for his mistake. A coworker is trying to charm you but you know something is fishy out there. A classmate appears to be cheerful but you have already sensed the hidden anxiety. For example, we often say that depression is faceless. People wear a smile in front of others but in reality, they are broken. While most of them around a depressed college fellow ignore her condition, you are sure that she is not healthy at all.

You need to link a person's emotions with his energy to get to know them better. Reading people by human vibe is all about decoding their emotions. By reading people's energy, you can bring yourself in line with how you relate to them, and whether you feel comfortable with them or not. If you study this subject and master it, you are able to make some crucial decisions in an effective way. For example, you will never want to spend your life as a spouse with a person who will drain your energy. The same is the case with a coworker. Why should you consume your time sharing your meals with a coworker who leaves you feeble and unproductive after a single sitting? That's why it is important that you learn how to read the human vibe.

Presence

The first thing to learn while reading people's energy is sensing the presence of people. This is the overall effect that a person leaves on you when he or she is near you. You have to calculate it. A girl in your office may leave mysterious, joyful or sad effects on you. Try to make out if the person around you is pulling you toward her. When you are reading them from their presence, try to notice if the energy they give off is warm or cold. Is it like fresh air or stalled? Do you sense anger or depression when you are near them? Whether it is a friendly sense or an intimate one when she is near you. On the basis of these readings, you can decide how to shape the future course of your relationship with that particular person.

Eye Projection

Another important method to read the human vibe is to take a closer look at that person's eyes. Eyes are the ways to transfer positive and negative energy. In Islamic civilization, eyes are considered as the source to transfer spiritual energy. Sufi poets like Rumi greatly focused on the importance of a glance. They say that the brain transmits electromagnetic signals through eyes. Looking straight into the eyes of your pet releases oxytocin which builds up a trustful and peaceful relationship between you and your pet.

You should take your time when you are observing her eyes, then study what kind of feeling you have. Is it the feeling of love, care, calm or anger? Do her eyes look sexy? Do they intimidate you? People's eyes may feel hypnotic at times. Sometimes looking deeply in their eyes make you feel insecure. That's why you have to study the effects of cautiously. If you come across a negative person, try not to engage them or they will zone in on you. If you sense positivity, keep looking straight into their eyes. Feed on all the positive energy.

Physical Contact

We share our energies with people upon touching them by means of a handshake or a hug. Whenever you touch someone through a handshake, you will know whether the person makes you feel comfortable or not. Or do you just want to withdraw? Do their hands feel clammy? This is a sign of anxiety. They will make you feel anxious. If they hold your hands in a powerful grip that your fingers feel pained, this gives off aggressive energy.

Voice Tone

Last but not least is the tone of voice in which people speak to you. It will speak volumes about their emotions and feelings. The frequency of our sounds creates distinct vibrations. Does their tone soothe you and make you calm? If you observe that the voice tone of a person is so soft that you barely hear him, this shows signs of low self-esteem. If they are too loud, this shows anxiety or insensitivity. If they are fast-talkers in your first meeting, they might want to sell something to you.

Try to observe if people are laughing too much. If this is the case, they are lighthearted. But their laugh ought to be genuine. (Orloff, 2014)

Chapter 5

Lies – Why They Affect the Way You Analyze People?

Lies go undetected more often, so do liars. Lying is quite prevalent among youngsters and this behavior hardly does any harm at that age, but when you grow older and enter professional life, liars can be harmful to your professional and intimate life. Kids consider this habit as something fun to tease their school mates and friends from the neighborhood. When they don't get caught, they consider this behavior as a way to go in life. They integrate this behavior into their personality and use it later on for personal benefits. So, that's how lying as behavior makes its way in our characters.

If you don't nip the evil in the bud, the kids will see this as a baseline for building up a powerful lying pattern to be used in the future. When you are dealing with these grown-up kids, you feel at a disadvantage because they maneuver it so professionally that you realize it only when they have already achieved their goals. It is not that liars are impossible to detect. In fact, they are pretty easy to spot around us. All we need are a few techniques to make out if a person is telling you the truth or is concealing something from you. Before we move on to analyze the techniques, we need to analyze different types of liars to make the process of detecting liars easy and smooth.

Types of Liars

Let's discuss the difference between people who are quite professional at lying. There are certain signs and symptoms that you need to watch out to find out what type of liar you are dealing with. Let's see and analyze each category to gain more insight when you are analyzing people.

Pathological Liar

The first category is the pathological liars. Pathological liars are habitual and they tell a lie in response to any kind of stimuli. They are very good at lying because of the magnitude of practice that they do. They are pretty good at fabricating stories and it is very hard to detect when they are lying and when they are telling the truth. If only you can read their facial expressions and gestures, it is easy to detect them. Look out for the movement of their eyes. If they are trying to avoid direct eye contact, they are not telling you the right thing.

If you want to understand why people lie so casually, you have to understand the circumstances they went through. They adopt pathological lying as a defense mechanism. It is a way to make their way through severe circumstances without hurting themselves. These are not excuses to become a pathological liar but these are the driving factors that push a normal person to integrate this personality trait. By understanding the pushing factors, you will be able to understand why people lie in the first place. In this way, you can stop a pathological liar midway while is weaving his web.

Sociopath

These liars are considered as the worst types of liars. They lie to achieve personal benefits without caring about how it will affect the people around them. They have a heart made of stone and they don't care about other people's emotions and even their lives. In simple words, they feed on lying. Lying is their strategy to get worldly benefits at the cost of the feelings and lives of other people. They don't feel shame or guilt at all.

When you are confronted with these kinds of people, you need to walk cautiously by carefully reading the situation. The situation can go out of control any time and you will find yourself becoming their victim in a snap. The reason is that they can turn out to be amazingly manipulative when dealing with you. They are experts in lying and they are more often quite cunning.

When you are analyzing these kinds of people, you are likely to end up reaching a wrong conclusion because of misleading or insufficient evidence. If you are currently into a relationship with a sociopath liar, you should try to free yourself of the commitment. When you are convinced that the relationship is poisonous because of the lying habit of your partner, end the relationship. You can exhaust your option of changing that person before taking a decisive step. (5 Types of Liars and How to Recognize and Deal with Each, n.d)

By now, you might be thinking that liars are like parasites who drain you of emotions and energy. But we must not forget they too are humans. They are not monsters whose only treatment is to send them in exile out in the wild or kill them with the best weapon available. It is advised that if you detect the lying habit in someone close to you for the first time, you should approach them with kindness. Show them love, tact and affection according to the size and impact of the lie that they just weaved for you or any other person. Don't forget to furnish your evidence or the other person will get away with it by denying it altogether.

It is highly likely that some liars will defend their lies and continue with it when you try to confront them, but you should keep in mind that liars have mastered the art of manipulation. Keep yourself in full senses to get away with their manipulation. (5 Types of Liars and How to Recognize and Deal with Each, n.d)

White Liars

We often see white liars around us. White lies are not real lies. At least they are not as lethal as real lies are. In most cases, they are perfectly harmless, and you can say that white liars more often tell one or the other kind of truth, that's why people believe that they are not lying. Some weak hearted people use white lies in a bid to protect themselves from the truth if they are of the opinion that truth will be damaging or hurtful for them.

When you detect white lies, you should approach those people and try to rectify their ways. If you find out that the white lie has insignificant value, perhaps you ought to let it pass. Otherwise, you can ask the liar to mend his or her ways as it is not a good idea to base a relationship on lies no matter how harmless the lies are. If you fail to detect white lies or let them pass as fun, they may cause serious problems for your intimate relationships in the long run. (5 Types of Liars and How to Recognize and Deal with Each, n.d)

Compulsive Liars

Compulsive liars are habitual when it comes to lying, but unlike pathological liars, you can detect them and figure out how to deal with them quite easily. They are not expert enough to weave a net of truth around their lies to make them appear credible to people. They are easy to analyze because they don't wear a cloak of truth over their woven web of lies. When they speak, you can tell that they are lying because they display such kind of behavior. Things to note when you meet such a person are that they will start sweating, and also they will never look into your eyes while telling a lie.

Compulsive liars can be further categorized into a habitual liar as well as a narcissistic liar. Habitual liars cannot refrain themselves from lying all the time. On the other hand, narcissistic liars make up stories about themselves. They tend to exaggerate things and like to embellish things about themselves. They will you stories how they confronted a dozen warriors and single-handedly defeated them. Other stories include how they turned out to be the hero of a number of situations like saving a girl from a raging fire. Most of the stories they tell may appear to be far-fetched. As per medical science, these kinds of people suffer from a narcissistic personality disorder. Lying becomes their habit because they feel deprived of their real lives. They have reached the conclusion that their real lives are boring and that no one is impressed with them.

How to Deal with Liars

There is a wide range of ways to deal with liars. This can be really difficult but the best approach is not to throw a fit of anger. The liar is likely to channelize your aggression toward diverting you from the subject. The best approach is to avoid getting carried away with their versions of events that you have concrete evidence of not being true. You can deal with liars by being polite and confronting them with the truth.

You have to understand the fact that all of us tell lies at one point or another. Sometimes we have to fabricate a lie to avert a crisis. Sometimes, you need to tell a lie because you don't want to hurt someone's feelings. These kinds of liars are easy to deal with because they tell a lie only to defuse a tense situation. White liars are also harmless unless they make it a habit to tell lies. What if you are confronted with a compulsive liar or a sociopath? They are habitual when it comes to telling lies.

Compulsive liars are not the easiest to deal with. In order to kill their sense of inferiority and inadequacy, they can go on to any extent to tell lies without caring for their effect on the lives of other people. They lack empathy and are unable to understand the extent of emotional turmoil that they bestow on the other people. Their dishonesty takes its toll on others. They are self-centered and can only think about their own benefit and profit.

These types of liars are the most difficult to deal with, but with greater understanding and practice, you can master the art. The first thing you should remember is to avoid confrontation with these kinds of people. They always try not to leave a trace of what they have done. When you confront them, they will come up with a new story to cover up their wrongdoing, in addition, they will become hostile in their attempt to invalidate your evidence. So, there is no point in confronting them. You have to make yourself believe that the person you are dealing with is not normal and he needs help. Think of him as a dysfunctional person who doesn't think normal. If you try to change them, they will resist any effort by hook or crook. So, you need to stop changing them. Just accept them as they are and deal with them as if they are normal. This will make them friendly toward you and it will be easier to deal with them.

The next step is to listen to what they say carefully. Don't trust it right away. It is better to retain the factor of doubt. Spare the room for verification of what they tell you. You should be careful about not letting them know what you are up to. When you are sure that the person is a compulsive liar, put a limit on the time that you spend with him; otherwise, they will keep draining you of energy and demoralize you.

These types of people don't merit your time and love. Avoid sharing your personal information and any other details with that person. Don't open up too much or they will use that information for their personal benefit. They can do that without thinking even once because of the fact that they don't have empathy for others. (Kloppers, n.d)

The next step you should take care of is that you must not expose a liar. You think that you have detected a liar and the liar also knows that. As per your impulse, you will rush toward your closest friends to tell them about that person in order to save them from his or her heinous behavior. Freeze and think for a moment. Is it really a good idea to tell others about him or her nature? The answer is a 'no.' In fact, it is pretty dangerous. The liar will behave like a suspect does on getting detected by cops. Move on in your lives as if nothing happened. Focus on what you are doing and you will be in complete comfort.

In some cases, if the liar is bent on inflicting losses and pain on you, you have to do something about it. Even in these situations, think about the possible impacts of exposing them. Better have a comprehensive discussion on the subject with the people who are close to you.

When you have decided to expose a liar, you should do this carefully so that you don't paint him or her in a negative picture. Try to convince others that he or she did that out of sheer necessity. This will paint your picture positively in the eyes of the liar. That's how you can expose him and also succeed in gaining his sympathy. In fact, this can promote friendship between you two.

In severe circumstances in which the chances of confrontation are high and moving on also is not a good choice, the only way is to show that you understand why the liar committed that wrong act. Not only show them by gestures or expressions but also try to tell them in clear words that you understand why they did that. Tell that it is normal to do that for self-protection, and also tell them that you accept them. That's how we are actually telling them that what they did was wrong but we are forgiving them. This has the potential to change their hearts. Perhaps they decide to mend their ways.

The above method doesn't always work. Some people tell harmful lies without shame or regret. They even inflict serious losses on people by telling lies. They are the ones who ought to be exposed so that other people should be saved from their lethal actions. You must not fear of exposing them and getting into a direct confrontation. They have already inflicted losses on so many people that there will be hardly anyone left who will show sympathy toward them. The people whom he has done wrong will support you. When we are done exposing them, we should immediately part our ways with them and become more cautious.

Compulsive liars are without a doubt hard to deal with. There is no hard and fast rule for the purpose. You have to read the person and then tailor your reaction to suit the circumstances. Without much homework, you will only land in trouble.

Chapter 6

Adverse Effects of Misreading People

This chapter is going to walk you through the effects of mixed signals. You will learn how people misread each other's signals and how it lands them in trouble or at least create a web of confusion among them. Reading people, though seems easy, is a tough nut to crack. If you miss out on a key signal and misinterpret it, you are going to misread someone's intentions. Bad intentions will be interpreted as good while good as bad. Similarly, wrong judgment will hamper our social connections or relationship with our colleagues.

This suggests that you should know the consequences of misreading people so that you may remain cautious. One wrong decision may land you in trouble. Mixed signals are dangerous in the sense that they confuse you, and confusion edges you off the right track. You should know what mixed signals are and how you can deal with them to avoid a crisis situation. This chapter also carries examples of mixed signals and the ways to tackle them wisely.

Mixed Signals

I have a friend named John who got a job at a grocery store. There he had a team of around a dozen people. As a good manager, he used to call a meeting every Thursday. Each meeting had an agenda that John followed in letter and spirit. John tells me that he wanted to be as handy to his staff as was possible. He used to help them in packing and putting groceries on the shelves for display.

John believed that he couldn't do more for the staff. Unlike most other bosses, John was a really good listener. He always welcomed criticism, suggestions and new ideas to improve the look of the store and boost sales. He was pretty satisfied with his role in the store. One day he welcomed criticism on his own performance in the store, so he requested his staff to criticize his shortcomings. Literally no one appeared at the meeting, suggesting that they had no issues with his style of running the store. After insisting for a week, one employee appeared in his office and opened up his heart. He said, "Mr. John, why do we think that we cannot do our jobs right. Why do you always come up to give us a hand? Don't you have confidence in our abilities?" This was completely shocking for John. He didn't think that his offer to help his staff would be perceived in another way.

John thought that by helping her staff, he would be able to identify with them. They will feel relaxed and satisfied, but the result was completely different from what he had thought. Instead of considering John a generous and kind person, his team felt a kind of inferiority complex.

This kind of scenario may happen and we don't even know about it. John's staff misunderstood his intentions. They perceived it as a lack of faith in their ability to do the job efficiently. These misunderstandings herald conflict as well as resentment, and this kind of misunderstanding is pretty common between couples. This story is also related to John. Compelled by his kind and affectionate nature, John wanted to hire a maid for her wife who was pregnant, and he did that accordingly. On the contrary, his wife thought that John didn't like the food she used to cook for the family just because he had passed critical comments on one or two dishes she had cooked. Despite the fact that you have explained that you are hiring the maid to relieve your wife of workload, but the seed of misunderstanding has already been sown.

Take a critical look at your own married life. There might be more than one occasion when you and your wife misunderstand each other for insignificant reasons. For example, you might be dining while your wife is telling a story to you. Although you are all ears to your wife yet she might find the act of your dining while she is speaking offensive. This may lead to a potential misunderstanding between you two. Similarly, you two have made a plan to go to a beach for sunbathing. Your wife feels sick and excuses herself from going with you. Although her excuse is genuine yet you might think that she doesn't want to go with you. Similar incidents of misunderstanding may happen when you two disagree on simple things like watching a movie together.

So, there is usually a big gap between what we say and how our listeners perceive it. The difference between real meanings and perceptions is not always a matter of egocentrism. Mixed signals are complex to understand but they have great importance when it comes to reading people. Mixed signals confuse you and land you in a blind spot where you cannot think clearly or see things how they are in reality. These signals cloud one's judgment of people and circumstances.

Take the example of a dating scene. You are dating someone who is not responding to your texts, but after some time, she reads your Whatsapp status or Facebook story. You will be confused. The point to understand is that we, as humans, lack perfection when it comes to expressing our thoughts. This is also true that we improve on our experiences and try to streamline our understanding of others' thoughts. Still, our true feelings tend to get hidden in how we translate them into actions and how we communicate through our speech. So, we can say that mixed signals are negative signals because that's how we are going to perceive them. One in hundred, if not thousands, will see something good in a mixed-signal.

So, should it go that way? Is it destined to be that way? There is an antidote to this problem. When you are confused about the inner feelings of a person, you should read their words coupled with their actions. But this demands practice, a lot of it, to decipher that hidden meaning accurately and perfectly.

Why Do People Give off Mixed Signals?

If you are receiving mixed signals, all burden is not upon you for reading her accurately. She also has to streamline lots of things. Mixed signals lead to miscommunication in most cases, and this affects the health of your relationship. Sometimes people intentionally use them to keep someone at arm's length because they just don't want to engage with them. For example, your fiancé is fed up with the relationship, but she cannot express it in words as it would be hard to hear and also, it would lead to an endless debate which she definitely wants to avoid. Here, she will start sending mixed signals to you. Like ignoring your texts but talking to you on phone or ignoring your call and responding to your texts, so that you take the hint that she doesn't want to be with you anymore. That's why first she will slow down the pace of the relationship and then she will say goodbye so that everything concludes making the least possible noise.

The story doesn't end here. Mixed signals don't always mean that the other person is trying to avoid you. It also is a way to cope with the stress that comes from getting intimated and close to other people. Your girlfriend might be going through this phase of stress, and you unknowingly end the relationship blaming her for intentionally avoiding you. Let's take a look at some mixed signals that sabotage relationships.

They Don't Meet up Your Expectations

There might come a moment in your life when you keep waiting on end for a special person in your life to respond to your texts or Whatsapp status. It is normal behavior to send and text and then expects a response to it right away. Absence of which can cause confusion and misunderstanding, and may mar your relationship in the long run. It is normal that the other person might be caught up in work. You will wait for the first few minutes but when a considerable length of time has passed, frustration will come to hit you hard. You will start feeling off about it.

It is possible that they will respond to you when they are free and when they find it convenient. In order to have a clear view of the circumstances, you should note if this kind of behavior has become a habit with them or not. One thing is clear from a recurrent behavior that the person is not fully dedicated to you.

Half-hearted Effort to Meet You

"I am dying to meet you. When will we meet? I am planning to drop in this weekend. Stay free." She texts you thrice a week but has not yet found time to come over on weekends and spend time with you. Every time she misses a weekend, she texts you saying that she remained busy. One or the other assignments keep her from coming over to you. She says that she has to juggle responsibilities and priorities. You remind her that she is placing other things as top priorities and ignoring you. People are not busy at all. It is all about priorities. When she has decided to meet you, she will find a way out. If she is not doing that, she has other things at top priorities. That's why she is unable to fulfill her commitment to you. Maybe she is sending you a mixed signal for a reason. Take the catch and make a decision.

She Doesn't Open up as She Should Be

When a relationship kicks off, you expect your partner to share everything with you like the names of her friends, information about her exes and lots of other things. It is this transparency that helps in cementing the foundation of your relationship. When the two of you have shared everything with each other, you will be able to form an emotional connection, which sets things off. Both you and your partner need to share their bit for a healthy connection. If you are sharing everything while she seems to be holding back, this is not a good omen for the relationship. The foundation will have cracks right from the start, which will eventually bring down the entire structure one day. Therefore, if you sense such a behavior, take it as a deliberately mixed signal. Analyze it and make a timely decision instead of delaying and regretting afterward.

Does Your Partner Flirt with Other People?

This turns out to be painful than other signals for lots of people, but this is also an important one to study if you want to make accurate assessments. This happens in thriller movies. The hero has a girlfriend who is a bit friendlier with his friends. At first, everything seems to be normal but slowly, you realize that she is up to something else. Do you remember a scene from any Hollywood movie in which hero plans for camping beside a lake along with his girlfriend and college fellows? At the campsite, she pays more attention to the friends of the hero. The hero gets confused at first due to the mixed signal. Then gradually, he realizes that something is fishy. His girlfriend is not actually interested in him. She is keeping all options open so that if one doesn't work out well, she could jump to the other.

The solution is not to frame allegations around her but keep patience. Ponder over how she is dealing with your friends. Note the dialogues, the gestures and the frequency of their meetings in addition to the time she spends with them. When you are sure that something is wrong, you should take her out for a walk at someplace where your friends couldn't reach to disturb you. Now you ask her in clear words about what is happening and why is it happening? You can request her to change her behavior because the current behavior unsettles you. If she truly cares for you, she will try to tone down her behavior and keep herself in check. If she doesn't try at all, take this mixed signal as a clear sign to make a decision. It is better to part ways than regret afterward.

She Cares for You When You Are Alone but Doesn't Show Affection When You Two Are in Public

Watch out for this mixed-signal carefully. She is ready to make out with you while you are at home. She is super comfortable while talking to you on end and watching a movie with you, but when you are out with friends for a hangout, she is unwilling to be seen with you. She just doesn't want to open up about her relationship with you. If your relationship is in its infancy, you should give your partner some time to adjust herself in your and her friend circles. When she is comfortable enough, the relationship will take a smooth road and move on well, but if she continues to behave like that after a while, you should take this signal with caution. Perhaps she made a hasty decision and now she is regretting. She may be pointing toward the underlying tension that exists in your relationship. Maybe she doesn't want to be seen with you anymore in public but is too polite to tell you so.

Remember that when a person truly loves you, their words and actions go on well. If she promises you to show up at your office when your boss throws a party for you and she doesn't keep it, these signals should be taken as serious. Like all other mixed signals, you have to give her some time. After three to four incidents, you will be better positioned to make a decision.

Chapter 7

Analyzing Verbal Cues

In order to know the difference between the truth and deception, you have to follow certain cues. The signs of lying are not clear; hence they are hard to understand. In addition, you cannot always be sure whether a person is lying or not. By practice, you can be able to tell if someone is lying to you or not easily. The rule is simple. When we are lying, we are deviating from how we behave naturally. We have to make an effort to look truthful while we are lying; that's why if you know how a person behaves naturally, you can easily tell when they are lying by tracing the difference in their behavior. The difference can be the inclusion of certain words or phrases that he normally doesn't use.

Look for Deviations in Their Words

Inconsistencies can help you distinguish the truth from the lie. For example, a person at your office tries to convince you that he didn't meddle in your documents. If he is telling the truth, he will not care what you like to listen to from him. Otherwise, he will formulate a plan in his brain. He will brainstorm what words and phrases should be used so that he may look truthful before you. The phrases like, "I didn't do that. I wasn't in the office at that time. How could if do it?" should be enough to put him under suspicion. In addition, he will repeat these words and phrases again and again. Experts believe that this kind of repetition buys them more time to think and fabricate another phrase that could convince you that he didn't do it.

Another verbal cue is that he will tell you more than you need to listen. Chances are high that he is telling you a lie. Liars talk too much because they have made it a habit to fabricate lies. They're uncalled for openness should be enough to alarm you.

Another indication of a liar is that they find it pretty hard to speak when you try to ask questions from them. They will stammer, lose words and find them entirely speechless. The reason for this kind of behavior is psychological. Their mind is not ready for rapid questions. Liars make up stories when you ask them a question. After one or two questions, they find them at a loss. Another reason is that our automatic nervous system malfunctions during stressful times. This dries them out of answers, which is an indication that they are telling lies. Also, watch out if they are biting or pursing their lips or not. Any such behavior is an indication of a liar.

Learn to Ask Right Questions

Parents have to believe what their kids say to them. When they say they were with their best friends whom you know very well, you believe them without investigating the truth. But when they tell the same thing again and again, this means there is something fishy in the bottom of the story. Teenagers want to do lots of things that pass their mind and to make it possible, they tend to tell lies to their parents so that you their parents or teachers approve of their activities. When they suspect that a particular activity would not be approved, they tell outright lies. This is the time to worry.

If you level allegation of lying against them, they will become hostile to you right away, and this will only make them more stubborn. That's why you need to be tactful to make them realize that their lie is not working without them knowing that you are manipulating them. That's where you need to use the technique of Volatile Conundrum. Try to create a scene. Ask your son the right question. Ask him where he went with Jimmy, the name he used to deceive you. Jimmy is his classmate whom you approve of if your son remains with him.

"You got home pretty late at night."

"Where did you go with Jimmy?"

He would say that they were at McDonald's to celebrate the birthday of their friend from school.

Here you have to come up with your own version of the story. "Really? I heard that a minute fire broke out at McDonald's due to short-circuiting. Did everything go well? When did the fire brigade reach the site?"

Now, this is the momentum where your son will be caught in a conflict. Whether to approve your version of the story or deny it altogether? If he approves of it right away in a snap decision, you have successfully caught a liar without confronting him. If he disputes the fact that the fire didn't break out but in reality it did, again you have successfully caught a liar. In this way, you have successfully put your kid in a Volatile Conundrum situation.

Knowing How and When to Read Verbal Cues

All of us use verbal cues almost every day. Have you ever wondered how do you communicate with people? What are the ways in which you communicate with them? Communication is not a simple process that you can easily understand. It is rather a complicated process that is so detailed that you cannot miss out on a single nuance without miscommunicating what you have on your brain. There are little things that you take into account during communication such as your reaction when someone tells you a joke. Whether you should laugh, smile, or don't do anything at all. We usually get ready to laugh when we are sure that the person has delivered her punch line of the joke. Some laughs are spontaneous. You just cannot wait to understand before you laugh whether it is the punch line on which you are laughing or not. So, that's complicated. What if you laugh before the punch line, would it not sound awkward? What if you have delayed the laugh? Now the other person will be in an awkward situation.

You have to look for verbal cues when you are communicating with someone. In communication, cues are generally considered as prompts that you can use to show others that it is time for them to issue a response or give a reaction. A verbal cue can be a word, a pause in language, rise in the tone or fall in it, or anything else related to speech. For example, I asked my friend,

"Shall we try our luck in starting a new business for the two of us?" Now I have put up a question for my friend and I expect a response from him. There should be an answer or the communication will hit a stumbling block.

Verbal cues are more important when we have to teach children at home or at school. Children are not so accustomed to understanding non-verbal gestures like facial expressions and body language. You have to explain everything in words before them. When a teacher has taught kids a lesson on the whiteboard. She asks them, "Can anyone draw a circle on her page like the one that is drawn on the whiteboard?" She will for sure use nonverbal gestures like pointing her hands toward the circle and toward the pages that are put in front of them on the desks. So, that's how with the help of clear words teachers are able to communicate their questions and instructions to the students.

Take another example. The teacher has taught the kids about circles and the way to draw them. They come the next day to the class. The teacher plans to take a surprise test about circles. She will draft a question in her head that will be easier for the kids to grasp and respond to. Perhaps she says to them, "You remember what we learned yesterday?" At least a few of them will respond in the affirmation. Now she says, "Who will come up and draw a circle on the whiteboard?" This is the question that the kids will understand and respond to you accordingly.

Direct and Indirect Verbal Cues

You need to know the words when communicating with other people. Direct verbal cues are clear statements or instructions. Parents are quite skillful in these verbal cues because they have to raise kids. Even new parents find out ways to train the children because verbal cues are integrated into our nature. Let's see some example of verbal cues that a child understands easily and integrate into his or her brain to use it in the future.

- Come to me.
- Go and clean your bedroom.
- What are you chewing?
- What are you studying?
- Why have you come so late from school?
- What are you thinking about?
- Have you brushed your teeth?
- Did you put the blender on the rack?
- Where are your books?
- How did your exam go last week?

So, these are the questions that we ask our kids every day. These examples contain clear instructions for the kids that's why they understand them right away and respond accordingly.

The second type of cues is indirect verbal cues. These also are considered as prompts but they are quite less obvious than the direct cues. I mean they are just not direct questions with a clear question mark at the end. When a teacher shows up in the class and puts the following questions?

- Has anyone seen my pen?

- Has anyone got an electric clock?

- Have you understood the concept well?

- Does anyone know how to draw a circle?

- Will anyone show up at the desk to draw a circle?

These questions are not specific to a single student. Instead, these are general questions. Only the students who will relate to them will respond to them accordingly. In simple words, we can say that indirect verbal cues throw the ball in the court of the listener. It is him or her who will decide whether to respond or not, how to respond and when to respond. The prompt in indirect verbal cues are not directed to any specific person. See the following examples:

- What are you going to eat today?
- What have you done from dusk till dawn today?
- What work have you done to clean the house?
- How did you bake the cake?
- How are you going to get a job in NYC?
- What are you going to do in the evening?

Chapter 8: Looking into One's Own Self

It is a proven fact that magic crystals, tarot cards, palmistry and astrology can help develop your psychic skills but still, the most direct and effective method to know about yourself is to connect with your own mind. If you really want to connect with your own self, you will have to invest considerable time in reading your habits and how you behave. Just like meditation, you have to stay away from television, radio, and mobile any other activity that would engage you to mind. There should be no children or pets around you while you are on your way to finding yourself. You can turn on light music if it helps collect your thoughts but you can also sit in complete silence if it makes you comfortable. Let's take a look at some key benefits of self-knowledge.

Benefits of Self-Knowledge

There are certain benefits that you need to take a look at in order to be motivated for exploring yourself.

- Knowing yourself will offer you a special kind of pleasure and happiness. You are in a position to tell other people who are. Your expression is confident and smooth. When you know what you desire for, you can express it in simple words.

- Knowing yourself helps you improve your decision-making. When you tend to know yourself, you are better able to make certain choices about the world. These can span from making small decisions to big ones like choosing your partner. You are more ready to tackle the problems of your life and also find solutions for them.

- Knowing yourself offers you self-control. The ability to know yourself helps you understand what motivates you to put a stopper to bad habits and what is needed to adopt good habits.

- Good knowledge of your own self helps you resist social pressures that are constantly mounting upon you from one or the other sides. When you know what you like and dislike, you are more ready to say yes and no to certain people and their proposals.

- This also makes you more willing to tolerate and understand other people. You are in a good position to know your own struggles which helps you identify with other people. This instills more tolerance in your personality. (Selig, 2016)

Let's see how you can know yourself.

Concentrate on Yourself

Before you go on to knowing yourself, you should clear your mind first of any intrusive or lingering thoughts that come to obstruct your mind. Bring yourself in a position in which you are the least distracted. Just focus on the current moment. You can try to focus on an imaginary point in your brain. Stabilize that point and try to find a grounding place where you find harmony. You need to focus on that point until your brain is free of negative thoughts. Concentrate on the white light of your consciousness. Feel the calm this state has brought to you. When you are no more distracted by negative thoughts, you can move on to the next step.

Ask Questions

Throw questions before your psychic self. This is where you can start thinking about your life and get answers from your own self. Before going into this procedure, you need to have a clear idea of what you have been trying to find out about you. It is always a better idea to jot down these questions on a piece of paper and memorize them. Now ask them from yourself. See the following examples:

- What is the perfect job for you?
- Where do you want to live?
- What type of partner do you want to have for you?

Try to be as clear as possible in asking questions. Vague questions will only produce muddled answers.

If you are doing it for the first time, it will be hard to get answers in the first go, so if your brain is empty of answers, don't take it to heart. Instead, keep trying to explore yourself. Give yourself time and space to settle on what you are trying to ask it. Keep your body and emotions in a fair check. You might feel unexplained sensations in your body or some emotional reaction. Don't ignore them. Note them down and try to see what they are trying to explain.

Gradually, you will be able to find the much-needed answers to your questions. Persistence and the right practice are keys to it. If you start curbing your emotions, you are binding your brain which is not good. Let every emotion and feeling flow naturally so that they may aid you in finding the right answers.

Know Your Personality

You should have complete knowledge of your personality. You think that you know yourself because you know who you want to meet, what you like in food and what you dislike, how you want your partner to be and behave. But have you ever experienced a situation in which you couldn't explain how you reacted in a certain way? We deal with certain people and things which we regret later on and even feel ashamed of. Still, we cannot explain why we reacted that way. How do you react to failure, success, a challenge or a bad day? All these things matter much.

Find out Your Core Values

Your core values, moral codes, and principles always remain dear and near to your heart. There are certain values on which you just cannot compromise. These values will ultimately affect your decision-making ability, the power to resolve conflicts, your way of communication and your day-to-day living style. Find out what they are by deep introspection, as I stated in details at the start of the chapter. Are they honesty, flexibility, integrity or security? Are you soft-hearted, dedicated to the cause of others, prone to learning, wise or a leader? Once you have agreed on what your core values, you be more than ready to analyze other people and also mend your own ways when you stray away from the right path. (be your own psychic – 5 steps to give yourself a psychic reading, n.d)

Know Your Body

Our body is as complex as our brain is. Whenever you start to know it, it changes. When we are children, it is pretty different than when we get old. It remains a piece of a mystery until death because we don't take an interest in exploring its limits. It is full of surprises. Sometimes these surprises are positive while at other times, they are absolutely shocking. Did you ever think what your breathing pattern is? What are your abilities? How flexible are you? How much balance can you bring in your walking pattern? (be your own psychic – 5 steps to give yourself a psychic reading, n.d)

There are times when we say no because our body has reached a certain limit. I cannot do this or I cannot do that. Our body feels challenged. Here you need to take the time to become intimate with your own body such as your strengths and weaknesses. Whether you are comfortable in cold weather or hot weather or balmy weather are things that you must know about you. Many people claim that they know themselves but in reality, they are missing out on clarity. They are just not clear about their mind and vision. (be your own psychic – 5 steps to give yourself a psychic reading, n.d)

You Need to Know Your Dreams

All of us have dreams of a great work future, kids and a luxurious lifestyle. We dream about so many things that we get confused which is the thing that we want more. What are our preferences? Knowing dreams are important and they are worth going after. Get to know them and prioritize them in your brain so that when someone asks you, you are able to speak about them clearly without stammering or repeating.

If you are confused about a dream, ask yourself if you want to do a certain thing. For example, you want to become an interior designer. Gather all the details about this profession. Now ask yourself if you can accept this profession with all its intricacies and liabilities. If you find the answer in affirmative, you need to integrate your dream in your daily pursuit of goals. If you find out that the dream existed in your mind without any reason and that you are not sure whether to pursue it or not, just discard it and never let it distract you in the future. (be your own psychic – 5 steps to give yourself a psychic reading, n.d)

Know What You Like

We believe that we know what we like but in reality this is not true. When someone knows himself, he is highly confident when dealing with others and doing some kind of work. The confidence is evident in his acts and speech. Almost every one of us gets carried away with the popularity of things thinking that we like them but the feeling wears away with time, leaving you confused.

Knowing yourself means that you know your likes and dislikes up to the extent that you are able to write them down on a piece of paper without thinking much when you are asked to do that. Ask yourself the following questions. (be your own psychic – 5 steps to give yourself a psychic reading, n.d)

- What are the foods that you like the most?

- Who are the people you like to meet more often or who give you a pleasurable feeling?

- Which fruits do you love to eat?

- Which vegetables are your favorite?

- Which family members make you feel comfortable when they come to meet you?

- Which friends are annoying to meet?

- Do you like mobile games?

- What type of clothes do you want to wear?

You need to start learning by looking into the mirror. Sort out what you like and what you don't. Now all you have to do is to stay true to your likes or dislikes. If you keep doing what you don't like and also ignore what brings you joy, you are doing great injustice to yourself. In fact, you have become ready to give up your own personality. In simple words, you are not going to be happy. On the other, hand, if you take care of your likes and dislikes, you are more likely to be happy. (be your own psychic – 5 steps to give yourself a psychic reading, n.d)

Practice makes you perfect. The more you practice, the better you will get on reading people. When you know yourself, you are better able to see others in a clear

Conclusion

Social cognition means how we understand people. This enables us to predict how they will behave and how they will share certain experiences. In addition, it is also critical that we understand certain nuances in everyday speech to make out the hidden verbal cues in the speeches of our colleagues and bosses. Many a time people don't mean what they say and don't say what they actually mean. For example, when someone says, "it is getting cold." It indirectly means that you should go and close the window or the door. You can easily understand the hidden meaning in the remark.

Practice makes us understand what is running in the minds of people, even if they don't speak it out. This is how we can understand their beliefs, experiences and feelings. When we place ourselves in others' shoes, we tend to learn how they think and will behave in a certain situation. This is the start of our understanding of our colleagues and family members.

Reading people is complex. Have you ever had a look at a person and figured out how that person thought or what his nature was? Did you reach the right conclusion? Or did you make a mistake right from the start? The conclusion doesn't matter. What matters is that you tried to make a judgment. If you are always right about your judgment, you are a lucky person because there are so many people in the world who have to go through lots of reading and practice sessions to be able to read other people perfectly. You always need this skill, whether you are an executive in a company who has to run a team of a hundred people or an employee who has to do lots of work and keep his boss happy. The need for reading people increases when you change a job or meet a new boss.

Only after a careful judgment of that person, you are able to better communicate with them.

Similarly, at home, you have to read the mood of your father and mother, especially when you have to communicate something important such as your marriage proposal, some girl or boy you like or about the future of work. Only when they are in a good mood, you can be able to say and be heard positively what you want to say. Perhaps you have scratched their favorite car so you will have to catch them in the right mood to communicate that tragic news to them. If you misread them, you will land yourself in great trouble.

Reading people is important and there is more than one reason for that to prove that this is a good skill to add to your skillset. Now that you have gone through the book, you can understand that reading people is essential before you approach a person to talk to him or her. If that person looks friendly, you can go on and open your heart to him; otherwise, you may decide to hold your feelings a bit longer. This skill can enable you to judge if your friend is upset. You can go on to know the reason of his disturbance and help him accordingly. If you are a master of reading and analyzing people, you are very well on the road to success at your workplace. You have to meet people who have different types of behavior. If you misjudge a cunning person and tell him your secrets, you have brought doom to your life by your hands. Similarly, if you have misjudged a sincere person and kept him at bay, you are missing out on a pure friendship that could have helped you climb the ladder at your workplace.

In addition, if you have to gain expertise in the skill of reading people, you are well on your way to be a social magnet. You can easily read people and judge the situation and tailor your communication accordingly. That's how you can win lots of friends and get popular in your social circles. For example, if people appear to be friendlier, you can approach them with a smile on your face and informal greetings. Otherwise, you can take up a formal persona and deal with them accordingly. So, reading people helps you take up a fluid personality that you can shape up according to the expectations of those around you.

This is a general rule. When you say things that others want to hear or behave as others expect you to do, you become a popular figure in your circles because you have mastered the art of keeping them in comfort zones those near you. Your social circles will remain full to the brim always. Understanding the feelings of others is an art that helps you anticipate what is running in their minds, which can help you tailor your speech.

The world is full of confusion. Misreading people leads to a flawed judgment that in turn leads to an inaccurate assessment. Sometimes, a misread facial expression can lead to cracks in the relationship and cause the death of it. For example, she loves you but just doesn't want to talk to you because she had a bad day at work, but you misread her facial expression and distance yourself from her. No matter how nicely she explains her position to you until you read it yourself, the element of doubt will remain in your mind. This small element can plague the entire relationship in the days to come.

So, reading people plays a crucial role in shaping up your intimate relationship. In addition, it can help you at your workplace. This book has walked you through the methods you can use to read people. These methods include reading people with the help of understanding their body language like the movement of their hands and arms, how they sit or how they walk. I have also explained in the book how you can read the facial expressions of a person to judge what he is thinking or what he has to say to you. You can read people by some pretty micro facial expressions to better your judgment of them.

A chapter in the book explained different types of people and different personalities that people take up to move through this life so that you have a better know-how of which type of personalities exist and what is the mindset that is linked to each personality. This will help you better judge people when you are able to identify them with a personality that you have read and integrated into your brain; the process of reading them gets smooth and easy. You also learned about the gut feeling and how it plays a crucial role in guiding your decision-making in day-to-day activities. In addition, you learned about the human vibe and how it can be linked to reading people. How you can study emotional energy and know how the other person makes you feel when he is close to you and how is he going to deal with you and whether you should keep in contact with him or not for the long term.

The book also explained different types of liars like what are their types and how they are you can deal with them. What steps you should avoid and what steps you must take to tackle them. You have learned the adverse effects of mixed signals if you misread them. Mixed signals have ruined lots of relationships and it continues to do so, just because we lack skills in sorting them out, and we always make a hasty decision.

I hope you have learned a lot and have started sorting out things in your brain. We have the basics of reading people in our subconscious. All we need is to sort it out by studying what a typical reaction means and then start implementing it on our social interactions.

References

be your own psychic – 5 steps to give yourself a psychic reading. (n.d). Retrieved from https://www.micheleknight.com/articles/psychic/psychic-ability/be-your-own-psychic-5-steps-to-give-yourself-a-psychic-reading/

Cherry, K. (2019). Understanding Body Language and Facial Expressions. Retrieved from https://www.verywellmind.com/understand-body-language-and-facial-expressions-4147228

Chu, M. (2017). The Truth About How Gut Instincts Really Work. Retrieved from https://medium.com/the-mission/the-truth-about-how-gut-instincts-really-work-d665425f1eb1

English, J. (2019). 5 Basic Body Language Signals of Manipulators. Retrieved from https://drwebercoaching.com/5-basic-body-language-signals-of-manipulators/

How To Read People Like the FBI. (2018). Retrieved from https://www.thrivetalk.com/how-to-read-people/

Kloppers. M (n.d). Dealing with Liars. Retrieved from https://www.mentalhelp.net/blogs/dealing-with-liars/

Orloff, J. (2014). The Power of Surrender: Let Go and Energize Your Relationships, Success, and Well-Being [pdf]. Retrieved from https://www.amazon.com/Power-Surrender-Energize-Relationships-Well-Being/dp/0307338215/ref=as_li_ss_tl?ie=UTF8&redirect=true&linkCode=sl1&tag=theminwor01-

20&linkId=7bec015a8cfbec80e5bb69f63a7c a784

Scott, R. (n.d). How to Read Body Language – Revealing the Secrets Behind Common Nonverbal Cues. Retrieved from https://fremont.edu/how-to-read-body-language-revealing-the-secrets-behind-common-nonverbal-cues/

Selig, M. (2016). Know Yourself? 6 Specific Ways to Know Who You Are. Retrieved   from https://www.psychologytoday.com/us/blog/changepower/201603/know-yourself-6-specific-ways-know-who-you-are

9 Personality Types – Enneagram Numbers. (n.d). Retrieved from https://www.theworldcounts.com/life/pote ntials/9-personality-types-enneagram-numbers

Made in the USA
Middletown, DE
16 December 2020

28412346R00086